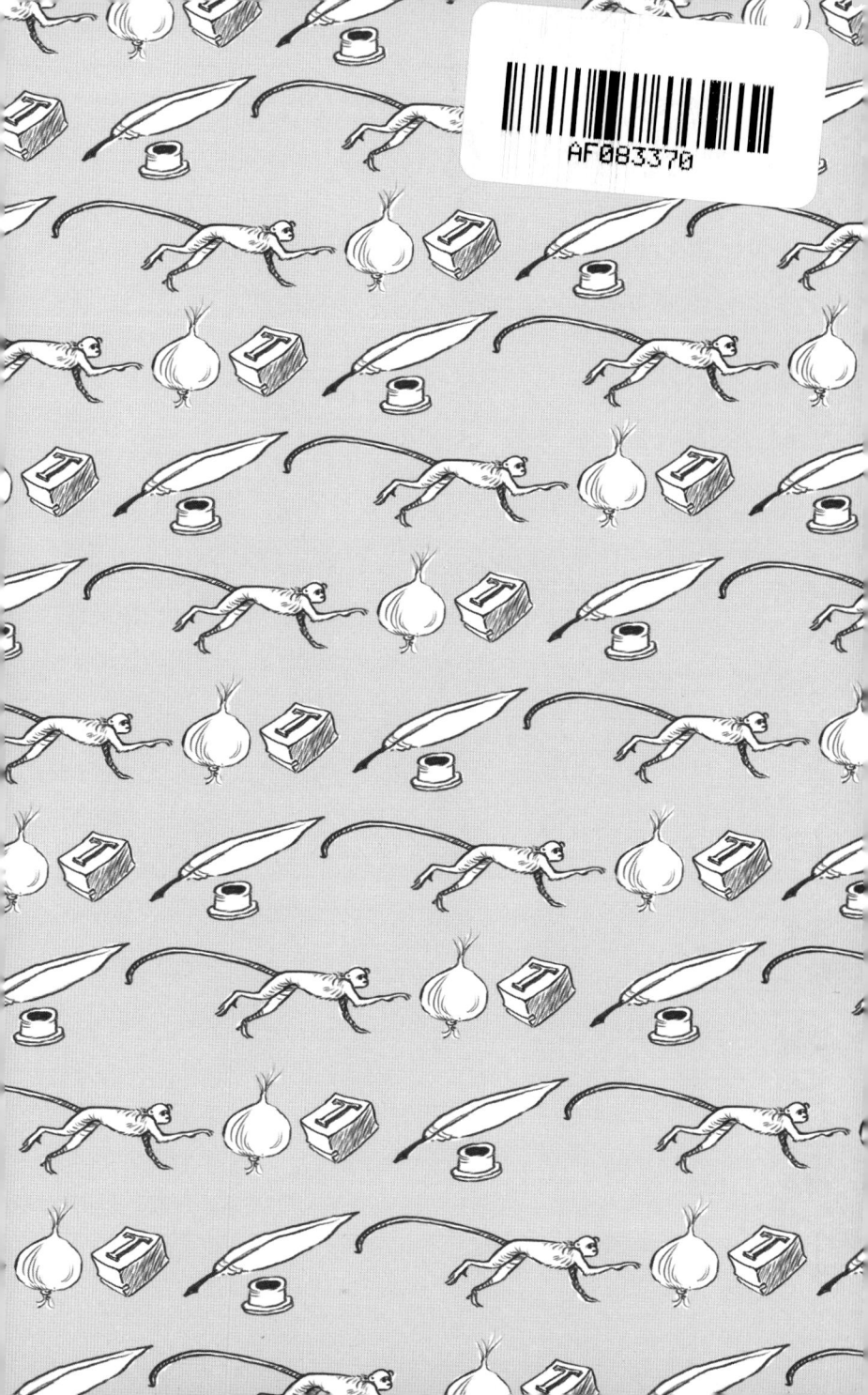

Tom Mitchell
Illustrated by Jon Davis

Shakespeare's
Monkey

Collins

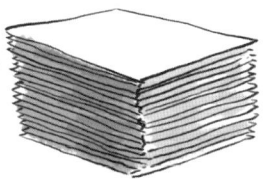

1. The new apprentice

"Close your mouth, boy. You're always gaping like a fish. Mind your manners too. And don't get your hands crushed by any of the presses. We've no money to pay master Griggs to clean up the mess."

In the weeks since Henry had been offered a position at master Griggs's print shop, this wasn't the first time his mother had given such advice. The difference today, however, was that it was Monday, *the* Monday, his first day. Here he was at the front door, nodding at his mother's words, taking the pie and apple that she'd tied up in a cloth, and stepping out into a new day.

He headed off from his home in Blackfriars, starting on the 15-minute walk across the city to Fleet Street, where the print shop, and many others, huddled near the shadow of St Paul's Cathedral. And, as he did so, he tried not to feel too nervous.

For once, Henry kept his head down and ignored all distractions: a miller arguing with a fish seller about something "wriggling" in their basket, hawkers shouting about the freshness of their oysters, a goose with a red ribbon around its neck, being chased by an old woman.

He was close to the print shop when two thin dogs raced out of a side street, directly across his path. Avoiding them, he caught his toe against a loose cobblestone. He tripped forwards but a passing sailor caught his elbow to save him.

"Watch yourself!" said the man.

It wasn't the stumble that unsettled Henry. It was the street itself. It was so full of people, even this early. It reminded him that today was his first day with grown-up responsibilities. His insides bubbled in protest at the thought. He was only 14!

"Early!" said master Griggs, as he unlocked the stout wooden door of his business. "How long have you been waiting, lad? In all the years of knowing your father, he's never once been early. How's he faring?"

"He's getting better. Slowly but surely. And I've been here since the rising of the sun!" said Henry brightly, though he'd only arrived a few minutes earlier.

"The rising of the sun, eh?" laughed Griggs and disappeared inside.

The print shop had been very different when Henry had last visited. This morning, he could hardly believe how quiet and large it was. The early sun streamed in from the huge windows, which were needed to keep the room well lit. And already the air was heating up! The cases of letters, collected in frames of sturdy wood, lined one wall. The movable type – square bits of metal, each making a letter – were fitted together to make words, sentences, whole pages. It felt like magic: a way to copy out any combination of words ever imagined.

There were three presses lined up in a row. Each of these could produce up to 250 pages an hour. He remembered the squeaking rhythm of them, the huge metal screws turned by hand. They were operated by two of the pressmen – one to ink the type (known as the "beater") and another to run the press itself.

Dark ink stained the wooden floorboards, the smell of many years of spillages hanging heavy. Henry knew that his hands, even his face, would soon stain similarly, for that's what happened to printer's apprentices. Pages of paper hung from criss-crossing lines, drying like laundry, and on benches across the space sat thick piles of yesterday's printed paper, waiting to get bound. It felt like the centre of something important, the brain of an inky monster.

Just for a moment, Henry felt a pinprick of panic. Maybe it was all too much? What would be expected of him? Compared to the thick oak trunks of Griggs's arms, his were twigs. Yes, he was far too young. He should be in bed.

He stepped backwards, towards the still-open front door. And, as he did so, he lost grip of his pie. It fell, he stooped to catch it, and his backside knocked against a mountainous pile of paper.

Instantly, he knew what had happened. He twisted sharply and caught the paper just as it had begun its shifting avalanche. With all his might, he steadied the pile and, as he did so, felt a bead of sweat run down the side of his face.

"Get your greasy fingers off that," said Griggs, returning from the storeroom, carrying a tin of ink. "We can't be selling spoilt prints." Henry moved to the printer, offering help. Griggs waved him off. "Seeing as you're the first here, I've a more important job than lugging ink tins. Set your food aside, young Henry … and tell me, have you ever set foot in a playhouse?"

2. The mission

Not that long ago, Henry's mother had sent him to the Globe Theatre with a penny and the instruction to be back before supper. "If you're printing plays with master Griggs, you should know what they're about."

He'd stood in the pit near the stage with the other groundlings and, to be honest, it had been difficult to focus on the play. He understood there had been mistaken identity between characters, but he couldn't follow much else.

Some lads, not much older than Henry, shouted and sang throughout the performance. When one actor appeared, they got particularly excited and threw hazelnut shells at him.

Henry had tried to move somewhere else, but the audience were so tightly packed that it was difficult. In short: not much fun.

"There's finally a good copy of *A Midsummer Night's Dream* that one of the actors from the Lord Chamberlain's Men has put together. It's going to be a big earner, Henry, and I need you to fetch it forthwith. The actor has been paid an advance already. He'll get the second half once I have the play."

"Me?" stammered Henry.

On his first day, he thought maybe he'd be cleaning the type or sorting paper into piles. Not collecting a valuable manuscript. What if he were to lose it?

"Who else can I ask?" said Griggs, glancing about the empty shop with exaggerated care. "We need that manuscript as soon as possible." He took a hand to the leather purse that hung from a belt around his waist. "Here's two pennies for the ferry across and back. You know where you're going?"

"The Globe, master Griggs."

"Good lad. Not far. Don't believe half of what you hear from the players. They spend their time pretending to be someone else, so they forget what real life is like."

Henry nodded, despite every fibre in his body willing him to tell his new boss that this plan was a bad idea, that he couldn't keep a loaf of bread safe, let alone a playscript.

Soon, however, he was feeling better. The walk up Ludgate Hill and down Paul's Chain to Paul's Wharf had been straightforward. And there was even a cooling breeze in the air. Sure, a few early street sellers attempted to get him to buy food, a woman begged for money, and a rat as big as a cat scattered across his path, but he made it to the river in good time. Here, the smell of fish and sewage coming from the Thames was enough to make your eyes water, but at least it was a familiar scent.

Bobbing on the river were several watermen, waiting for passengers in their small boats, calling out destinations. Noise, noise, noise. Henry had forgotten how much shouting there really was in the city.

"To Bankside!" called one man with a big smile and, given there were already some passengers in the boat, and it would likely leave soon, Henry stepped in and offered his penny.

The wherry, a type of narrow river ferry, wasn't much bigger than a rowboat.

There were three others aboard, including a child younger than Henry who held two chickens, and another waterman to help with rowing. Henry kept his head down and tried to ignore the boat's rolling, the smell, and the cackle of the chickens.

This he managed and, within 15 minutes, he was on the far side of the river. Five minutes after this, Henry stood outside the Globe. Easy! And to think he'd been worried about being a printer's apprentice!

The theatre loomed like a huge, wooden crown, plonked down among the cookshops and bear pits of Bankside. And no longer did Henry have to ignore the stink from the Thames. It had been overtaken by sweat sawdust and rotting vegetables. He remembered this combination from when he visited before.

At this time in the morning, the street was empty of the bustle you'd expect of an afternoon, when the plays were performed. Now: to business. But where to go? The main entrance, two wooden doors set in the white and timber walls, were closed.

"Boy! You!" The voice came from a man who'd stuck his head out of a side door.

Henry pointed at his chest and mouthed "Me?"

"Why, of course, you! Don't dally. Come through this instant!"

The man disappeared.

Who was he? Did he have the play? Or was Henry in trouble? The only way to find out was to follow.

3. The Globe

Through the door was a dim passageway and no sign of the shouty man. Behind the walls, close to both shoulders, rumbled sounds – voices, stamping, laughter. The day had already offered its share of bad smells. This place was no different. Was that the smell of wet cat? Candle smoke? Something sweet and rotten – old fruit, maybe? He should watch where he stepped.

At the end of the passageway was a door. Henry pushed through and stepped into a dim, narrow space that extended right to left. The same whitewashed walls were here, with low wooden beams criss-crossing the space. This was backstage, the "tiring room", where actors got ready for their performance. He paused. Hanging on the wall opposite – was that a lion's head? And beside it, a pair of wings? On the shelf below, half a dozen crowns. Below all this were three wooden crates, each overflowing with bright fabric.

"Where's my dagger? I need a dagger!" A man in a doublet pushed past Henry. "Stop gawping, boy, and assist the search."

Henry stepped towards the chests, making like he was looking, until the man continued off and away. Thinking it best to go in the opposite direction, and ignoring the frantic beating of his heart, Henry passed through as the space opened out into a room. There he found six people. Two were wearing togas, one had a flowing shirt. Another was lying flat on the floor. The other two – costume assistants, judging by the needles and thread – barely looked up.

The man on the floor flicked through pages of a book. Was this Henry's manuscript? No, it was bound.

"It's 'lend me your ears', not 'deers', you clod," said the man, addressing an actor in a toga.

Henry felt a hand on his shoulder. "I've been calling you. Follow me. You're Griggs's boy, yes?" It was the man from earlier.

Before Henry could reply, the man had already vanished again, off through a curtained door on the opposite side of the room. *Actors! Always so dramatic.*

When Henry pushed past the curtain, he almost knocked directly into the man, who was waiting in the gloom of the other side. He spoke with a low voice. "And the coin, boy? I've had the first half – now show me the second."

Henry thought back to what Griggs had said. "Master Griggs instructed me to say you'd receive the second instalment, following – "

The actor put a finger to his lips. "Yes, yes, yes. But I'd hoped – "

And, as if conjured from nothing, a thick stack of papers appeared in his hands. He passed them over heavily to Henry.

The same thought occurred to both of them.

"You have nothing in which to carry the script?" asked the actor. "There'll be trouble if I lose money due to a child's greasy hands."

Henry just blinked. Why hadn't Griggs given him a bag? Had it been a test?

The actor rolled his eyes. "Oh, the trials I endure! Surrounded by amateurs! Wait thee here!" He swept back through the curtain.

Henry gripped the playscript as tightly as a baby gripping their parent's hand. And his hands *weren't* greasy. Why did people think they were?

"How long have you been in master Griggs's employ? Manuscripts need bags, boy. Do you realise how valuable this is?"

The man now held a cloth bag. He took back the papers and, with a sweeping flourish of his fast hands, slipped the manuscript into it.

"Now, you tell master Griggs that this is the finest copy of master Shakespeare's *A Midsummer Night's Dream* that exists anywhere in England. Taken directly from the players' mouths." Henry nodded. "Are you one for the theatre?"

"I like the ones about history."

"Excellent, excellent … well, I expect you'll be wanting to get on your way. The sooner you reach your destination, the sooner I receive full payment." He lowered his voice. "And should you happen to run into the master Shakespeare himself, pretend this is nothing but a collection of your grandmother's recipes. Understood?" And then the man frowned and leant in closely to better see Henry's face in the thin line of light that emerged from a high window. Henry would have pushed him away, but his hands were full. "Have you ever considered the stage? A dab of rouge and the right wig – we'd have you weeping as Juliet in no time."

"I'd rather not," said Henry, nodding farewell at the actor, and rushing back through the curtain.

"And ensure you return that bag!" called the actor. "Honestly, coming here without even a –" His voice trailed off. Henry had gone, and he no longer had an audience.

4. Monkey business

Stepping out of the theatre into the bright Bankside morning, Henry allowed himself a smile. That hadn't been so hard, had it? With the playscript tucked safely away, all he had to do now was catch the ferry and be back in the shop within the half-hour.

What next? Master Griggs might even trust him with something more challenging than sweeping the floor. He'd proven himself. What a first day! Just wait until he told his mother – although she'd never believe it.

Grinning even wider, he spotted a small crowd up ahead. There was time to stop, wasn't there?

If only he had more than the single penny for the ferry.

In a small square, a short man stood on an upturned box, cloaked entirely in black. The cloak swamped him – its sleeves flopped over his hands, which he shook to better display a small bottle of medicine. But that wasn't the oddest thing: perched on his shoulder sat a monkey in a tiny red hat. It made him think of Mrs Seymour, from upstairs, who'd kept a monkey and insisted it reminded her of her long-dead husband.

"And I promise on everything I hold true and value that two drops of this liquid a day kept my dearly beloved father alive until the age of 103."

He was a mountebank – some called them quacks. Henry's father had warned him about them – they'd stop you in the street and make all kinds of promises about everything. Cures for any illness, potions to make you grow taller, ways of guaranteeing good fortune. Their only truth, however, was that they wanted your money.

The crowd was made of about a dozen people, positioned around the speaker in a horseshoe. These weren't interested customers, though. They'd stopped to be entertained by the seller's outrageous claims.

"As if!" called a man. "When did your old man die?"

"Why, 103," the mountebank repeated. "And he'd have lasted even longer if not for his legs."

"I meant the year," replied the man.

"Let us not tangle ourselves in the vines of dull detail. Tell us, kind sir, do you have a wife?"

"Well … I'm not of the mind that's – "

The mountebank lifted his bottle. "Two drops of this in your beloved's eyes and the first thing she looks upon, she will fall instantly in love."

"Really?" asked the man.

"Mark my words. Not only that but – "

And as the mountebank began to list the potion's further incredible qualities, not least the ability to turn lead into gold, Henry's attention moved with the monkey. It had jumped down from the mountebank's shoulder and skittered across to the crowd, who, as one, had begun to take the mountebank a little more seriously.

The monkey paused at the feet of a man who wore a rich wool doublet and lace collar. Over his breeches was a leather belt and, from this, hung a dagger and a purse. The monkey stretched an arm and, with a practised flick, snatched the purse clean away.

"Sir!" Henry shouted. "That monkey's got your purse!"

The man reacted quickly, grabbing the monkey and pulling the purse from its desperate fingers. It was a clever monkey and knew when to give up.

"Banbury!" called the mountebank. "It's rude to steal!"

"That's not even your monkey," said someone.

"It belongs to a sailor. How can we believe a single thing you say?"

"'Tis true, I'm borrowing the beast from a Portuguese sailor," said the mountebank. "Not everyone can pay for an apprentice, you know."

Banbury wasn't listening to any of this. Instead, he was tiptoeing towards Henry, who edged back, heart thudding. The monkey had a look in its eye.

"Banbury!" called the mountebank again. "Leave the tell-tale be!"

Banbury looked over his shoulder, then turned back to Henry. And Henry, it's fair to say, was not feeling especially kindly towards the animal. The threat of being bitten by a monkey tends to sour one's mood. Still, even if he had wanted to act, there was no time – the monkey had already launched itself at him. Not to attack, as it turned out, but to swipe at the bag slung over his shoulder. Henry stumbled, arms flailing, and crashed onto the cobblestones. His bag slipped free and its papers spilt out. Banbury scampered

through the mess, seized a fistful of pages and disappeared into the forest of legs.

"That monkey's stolen my play! Somebody seize that monkey!"

As Henry was helped to his feet, Banbury scuttled away from the bustle of the square, off towards an alleyway. A kindly woman slapped the bag and what remained of the manuscript into his chest. "You'll not want to be forgetting this."

Henry, already starting after the monkey, could see there was a good quarter of the play gone. Banbury had taken the play's final act. And what good is a story without an ending? Imagine what master Griggs would say!

Reaching the alleyway, Henry had to dodge someone throwing dirty water from a window, and another searching through an abandoned punnet of rotten apples. He sped along the cobblestones and, as the alleyway led to a marketplace, he paused, scanning the riverside market.

And there, on a barrel, sat Banbury – cool as you like – nibbling at a sticky, half-eaten honey cake. The monkey saw him and scarpered.

Stallholders were setting up for the day and there was the smell of fresh fruits and baking bread. Near where he'd seen the monkey, Henry skidded on something cold, wet and probably once alive. He didn't look down.

"Thief!" shouted someone and Henry felt something hard strike his back. It was probably a rotten potato, it certainly smelt like one, but he had no time to stop and check.

"It's not me! It's the monkey!" he called, passing between the last row of stalls and almost having a nasty accident with a low washing line and a pair of breeches.

There was a flash of red in the corner of his eye. He turned. Was that the monkey disappearing into Clink Street? He had no option but to follow, his chest now burning with the exertion. He scolded himself for ever thinking being a printer's apprentice would be easy.

A grimy hand shot out between the bars of a window. "Got any pie, lad? Or keys?"

The Clink prison! The foulest of all foul places to end up. Sprinting along the narrow street, with its tall, dark brick walls either side, Henry ignored the prisoner, head peering between the bars of his prison.

And there! At the end of the street, another flash of red, turning left. Henry upped the pace, knowing that if he didn't return the script, Griggs would surely dismiss him.

5. Going in circles

As he turned left out of Clink Street, hot on the heels of Banbury, Henry saw the warehouses and wharfs of the Thames. And with this vision came a feeling, a sinking feeling, a why-does-nothing-ever-go-right-for-me feeling.

He'd run in a loop, circling back on himself. Up ahead, back a little from the river, was the Globe. And also: no sign of the monkey.

"You're a sight, you are!"

Henry turned to see a young boy in a princess costume, holding a wooden dagger. He was sitting on a low wall with his back to the water. Below him, on the exposed sand of the river, scavengers combed the gravel and sand for anything of value that might have been dropped.

"You haven't seen a monkey, have you? Small, red hat, very fast?" asked Henry.

The boy in the dress, who couldn't have been much older than Henry, shook his head. It really was an amazing outfit. Were they pearls?

They couldn't be, surely? And if not for the knowledge of the many and troubling punishments that would be awaiting Henry at the print shop if he didn't return the manuscript by sundown, he might have been tempted to ask whether they had been made specially for the play. For clearly, this was an actor. Women weren't allowed to act so, instead, young men took their roles.

"A monkey, you say?"

"Banbury. He was with a mountebank, a quack with a bottle of fake medicine. Up that way."

The young actor looked to where Henry pointed. The crowd had dispersed. The quack had gone. There was no sign of a monkey.

The actor finished his apple and, without looking behind him, chucked the core over his shoulder. Down below, it only just missed a red-faced man with a huge sack.

"Have you spoken to Jim?"

"No," said Henry. "Who's Jim?"

"He's the keeper of the bears at the bear pit. George and Ned are his bears. Ghastly animals. Anyway, they are notorious for hating monkeys. Can't stand the beasts. A Portuguese sailor brought one to the pit a week or so ago. A particularly cheeky fellow. The whole place near came to ruin. The bears went wild. If there's a monkey on the loose around here, you should speak to Jim. He tracks them all."

"Yes!" said Henry. "Thank you! The mountebank mentioned a sailor!"

He took a deep breath, then set off in a run towards the Beargarden.

6. Trouble at the press

Meanwhile, not far from Griggs's, master Filbert slouched in the doorway of his print shop. His business was a smaller, stinkier version of Griggs's and he absolutely hated his rival for exactly this reason. Filbert was prone to sharp headaches and a sharper temper. The constant rattle of the type and press drove him to despair. He was a thin man with a thick beard and a nose that looked like a raspberry.

"Excuse me, master Filbert."

Filbert turned from watching a pair of stray cats fight over a rotting cabbage. Behind him, on the threshold of the print shop's gloom, stood his apprentice, Boggins.

"What's the matter, you stewed prune?"

Boggins didn't even flinch. He was used to Filbert's language.

"*A Midsummer Night's Dream*, master Filbert. There are reports that a good copy is on its way to Griggs's shop. A boy picked it up from the Globe, not 15 minutes ago."

Filbert growled. At this, Boggins whimpered.

"What have I told you, sirrah?" asked Filbert.

"To wipe my nose and avoid looking you in the eye, master Filbert."

"About our rivals. About his name."

"Never to mention it, master Filbert."

"Too right, never mention it. The man's a charlatan. He only occupies his position because his mother was a handmaid to Lord Burghley's wife. And you know what that lot are like."

"Aye, master Filbert. The boy. You'll recognise him. He's master Oates's son."

Filbert remembered Oates. He'd been ill recently. Poor man. But it served him right for associating with Griggs.

He turned back to the street. The cats had finished fighting. One sat chewing at the brown cabbage, the other sat a little off, licking its paws and looking particularly sorry for itself.

A good copy of one of master Shakespeare's most popular plays? How did Griggs get his hands on that? Well, the answer was quite obvious. He had cheated somehow. Filbert imagined the smug man, sitting on his smug chair, as his smug presses printed smug copies of the smug play. It was a play, Filbert had to admit, that he'd never seen the attraction of. A fairy queen in love with a donkey? Ludicrous.

He stroked his beard, lost in thought. What if he got the manuscript before Griggs? What if he were the one to print it? Not only would he make some much-needed money, but he'd wipe the grin from his competitor's face.

"Boggins! Tell Brooks to watch the press. I'm off to make us rich."

7. Bears and brawls

The Beargarden was like the Globe, if the Globe had swapped speeches for teeth. Instead of watching a play, you came to watch bears fight dogs. Henry had never seen the attraction. He wouldn't say that he liked the grizzly animals, but the idea of chaining them up and watching them fight made his stomach twist.

Big Jim's two bears were locked in a wooden pen, a huge kennel with iron bars, in the filthy rear courtyard of the Beargarden. Henry watched a boy, about the same age as himself, unlock it. He held a wooden bucket, and its contents – meat a local butcher didn't want – absolutely stunk.

Henry couldn't see the bears. But because of the way the boy moved, and the occasional clinking of their irons, he knew they were in there.

"Nice to be talking about something other than bears," said Big Jim. "When you keep bears, the only thing anyone ever wants to talk to you about is bears. It gets boring." He lowered his voice. "Truth be told, I can't stand the creatures. Never wanted the job."

"So why did you become a bear keeper?" asked Henry, eyes on the boy in the cage.

"My father was one. And his father. And his. It's a family tradition. Monkeys, though! I love monkeys. Could talk monkeys until the setting sun."

A deep growl tremored from the cage. With a sharp crack of a dropped bucket, the boy came running out, closing the pen shut behind him and pulling across the bolt.

"Stop acting the goat, Thomas!" said Big Jim. "And fetch them water to wash down their meaty breakfast."

Thomas, with a face the colour of a ghost, nodded and wandered away.

"This monkey," said Henry, conscious that the longer he spent here, the further Banbury was likely to travel. "He's stolen something valuable. An actor I met told me you might help."

"Something valuable, eh?"

"The monkey was with a mountebank. Not far from here. He tried stealing a gentleman's purse."

"Speak true: was the little beast wearing a red hat?"

"He was! He was!" replied Henry.

"Some time past, a Portuguese sailor caused trouble by bringing his monkey here. And if there's one thing my bears can't stand, it's monkeys. The crowd chased the two of them, the sailor and his hairy acquaintance, away. I heard they escaped on a wherry across the Thames. If you want to find your hairy thief, he's the other side of the river, in the sailor's lodgings. I'm told some customers chased him all the way there!"

The other side of the river! Not ideal but at least it was a clue. And one that brought him closer to master Griggs's print shop.

"What troubles thee? You're gaping like a mooncalf."

Henry closed his mouth. He must continue the chase! He nodded to Jim. "Thank you for your help."

Big Jim nodded. "Like I said, it's good to speak about something other than bears."

Thomas appeared with a bucket of water. "Master," he said. "Might you bring the bears their drink? I'm of the opinion that they don't like me."

There came another growl but this time it was from Big Jim. "The cheek! Get to it, boy! Or you'll be out of work again!"

Maybe, thought Henry, *ink-stained fingers were better than being breakfast for a bear.*

8. Hope floats on the Thames

How big is London? How many people live here? Henry remembered his father saying it was something like 200,000, nearly as many people as lived in Paris. It was so large a number, it wouldn't fit in his head. But walking back to Bankside, the narrow path full of the bustle of early morning London, he could well believe it.

At the wharf, he was struck by a wave – not from the Thames, but the surge of movement and noise around him. People were getting into boats, getting out of boats, shouting destinations, arguing, chasing chickens, asking for money, warning dogs. He wouldn't admit it to anyone, but his eyes watered once more and not because of the strange eggy smell that wafted from the river. It was all a bit much.

He found a waterman with a boat heading for Paul's Wharf and, after handing over his penny, pushed through to step into the rolling boat. He sat down on the thwart, one of the wooden benches that stretched across the boat, joining the other passengers.

And he waited. And he continued waiting. The other passengers didn't seem bothered. The waterman continued shouting, "Paul's Wharf! Paul's Wharf!" like they were the only words he knew.

At that point, his panic gave way to something worse: the dull certainty that he'd never find the monkey. His first day as a printer's apprentice would also be his last. He felt sick.

"You'll catch flies with your mouth open like that," said a woman with a sleeping baby, sitting alongside Henry.

He closed his mouth.

"Master boatman?" said Henry, turning his attention to the boat's owner. "Will we soon be leaving? I'm attending to urgent business."

The waterman stared down at Henry from the stern, where he stood to shout at potential customers. He didn't reply.

"He won't leave until every space is filled," said the woman.

Henry nodded and let his attention wander to the water. This close to the shore, there was all kinds of floating rubbish. Among the rotten vegetables and fish heads was a limp rat, on its back, as if sunbathing in the brown water.

And there! Something else! A scrap of paper. A scrap of paper exactly the same size as those sheets in his cloth bag. Henry leant over the side, the gunwales, and stretched to grab the paper. The boat rolled to the side and the waterman very nearly fell in.

"Watch what you're doing, boy!" called the waterman, proving he did have more language than the phrase "Paul's Wharf".

Henry offered a quick apology but the danger of upsetting big-armed, menacing men wasn't his focus. He leant over the side of the boat again, and this time he managed to scoop the page out of the grimy water.

Although the ink had run, he could read enough to see that the paper in his hand was from *A Midsummer Night's Dream*, his *A Midsummer Night's Dream*. It was the last page!

"What's that?" asked the woman.

"Umm ... it's a page from a comedy by

master Shakespeare," said Henry, brain whirling, sickness fading.

The woman sniffed. "I saw his last one with the donkey. Never understood how people liked that," she said. "A donkey wooed by a fairy queen? Pah!"

But Henry wasn't listening. The monkey had obviously crossed the river not that long ago. As long as Banbury hadn't dropped any more pages, Henry might still be able to save the day.

And if he had to write his own ending for the play, he would. I mean, it couldn't be too hard, could it? Unlike many people, Henry knew his letters and could easily make something up about donkeys and fairies.

Yes, thought Henry, as the waterman finally took his position at the oars, *I'm on the right track. The day isn't lost yet!*

And as the wherry finally began its crossing, arriving from the opposite bank, was Filbert. He'd spotted the boy, of course he had. And as soon as his boat had made land, he scrambled into a return ferry, barking at the boatman to push off at once.

9. The writer and the clue

Back on the north shore, Henry had done his best to dry the soggy page, using a sleeping dog, of all things. The fur made it harder to read, but what else could he do? He'd not be parting with it now.

So, what now? The proximity of Griggs's shop had started off his nerves again. His only clue was that the monkey might belong to a Portuguese sailor who might live somewhere this side of the river.

Not hugely helpful. Still, he had to at least try to find the monkey and given that the script didn't look like it had been in the water for very long, Banbury might even be nearby.

What Henry didn't know was that, as he wandered into the city, Filbert was jumping from his boat, already out of breath as he began his pursuit of the boy.

Henry glanced up at the roof of St Paul's Cathedral. What if the monkey had climbed up there? That's what monkeys do, after all. He decided that it would be better to face the wrath of his master than try scrambling up.

This part of town was the centre of London's book trade. The bustling, open space around St Paul's Cathedral held dozens of booksellers – some with fixed shops and others with open-air stalls, lining the walls of the courtyard. There were even publishers and stationers, some of them master Griggs's competitors. It felt cruel that he should find himself here, a reminder of how much trouble he was in.

"Poetry is wit, not rhymed nonsense written by the uneducated and donkeys!"

Standing in front of a stall, a man waved a pamphlet in the air. Although the stall-owner listened patiently, the words were aimed at the passersby. This was Ben Jonson, a playwright and poet. Henry recognised him because his father had once pointed him out. He'd been standing on a barrel in Bankside reciting a poem about how he'd been hoodwinked by a turnip salesman.

Jonson was a stout man, with cheeks the colour of cherries. He had thick, dark hair, a wiry beard, and eyebrows that looked like they could crawl off his face and start a fight of their own.

"Please, master Jonson!" said the bookseller. "There's no need!"

"Of course there's a need," said the writer, turning again to the market. "A man is shown through his language. And this here – " He indicated the pamphlet he held – "not only shows a lack of wit but is sufficient to rob the reader of theirs too."

Jonson held the pamphlet up to a passerby, who nodded. But Jonson continued: "You'll be as well to commission the monkey you found so entertaining to write you verse. The outcome would be better than what we have here. A monkey!"

There was some laughter from the few people who'd stopped.

"We liked the monkey!" called someone.

"A testament to your intellect. A thieving little beast with a taste for candied peels. Ha!

More popular than men of letters! Tell me, do you have your letters? Can you read?"

He couldn't mean Banbury, could he? A monkey that steals? This was surely not a coincidence.

Candied peels? Henry turned to look around the courtyard as Jonson argued with the man.

And there, yes, he saw a confectioner's stall. Breaking into a jog, he darted over. And, on a barrel, he saw a smear of sugary handprints. Monkey fingers! On the cobblestones, a half-chewed, syrupy orange peel – ink smeared!

"Candied fruit? Peels? We've lozenges and comfits too," the stallholder said.

But Henry didn't reply. He was already off. Because there, up ahead, had flashed a red hat.

Banbury.

"The youth of today!" said the stallholder, staring after Henry. "Mark my words – no good shall come of lads like that!"

10. The market chase

East of St Paul's Cathedral was Cheapside, London's main thoroughfare. Here were more stalls and it was now late enough in the morning for them to be bustling. There were different areas for different foods. Henry knew the areas well from visits with his parents – usually a place for spice samples or gawping at oranges from Portugal and Spain. But today, he had a monkey to catch. He tried not to consider how close to the print shop he was.

Henry had to watch where he stepped – and not just because of the discarded food – there were huge piles of horse dung, and children nipping through the crowd, between the two rows of stalls, searching for loose purses to pluck from belts.

Despite Cheapside's frantic busyness, Henry sensed he was close. Focus: that was what was needed. The sort that made for successful printer's apprentices.

And yes! There! A flash of monkey – moving between stalls selling eels and lampreys.

"Mind thy path, boy!"

A pie-seller, holding a crate of steaming pies, stepped directly into Henry's path. The wooden edge of the crate had thumped him in the ribs and sent him flying backwards – just missing a pyramid of horse dung by a hair.

"Thief!" shouted someone and the pie-seller narrowed his eyes to focus on Henry.

Why does everyone think I'm a criminal? thought Henry.

But Henry soon realised the voice couldn't be referring to him. It was coming from further down the street.

The pie-seller moved on and Henry got up.

"That monkey!" called someone else. "It stole my onions!"

What was it with Banbury? Henry thought. *Did he have some need to steal everything he came upon? Or was he working under instruction? Had the Portuguese sailor sent him out with a list?*

Henry burst into a run, dodging a barrow of sprats and herrings, the smell knocking him sideways, nearly tipping it over as he brushed past. A child chasing a hoop veered into Henry's path, and he was close to turning his ankle as he avoided her. And, naturally, there was a stray dog, barking and snapping at Henry's ankles as he ran, before being distracted by a dropped onion.

There was a flash of red under the low eaves of a timber building and down an alleyway, and Henry turned to follow. It wasn't far to the dead end and there, on a messy pile of broken barrels, sat Banbury. He looked as if there was nothing unusual about the morning, as if relaxing there with a string of onions in one hand and, a wedge of papers in the other, was a natural thing for monkeys to do.

How was he still gripping them all – he must hold master Shakespeare in the highest regard!

Henry tiptoed forwards, slowly panting. He didn't want to spook Banbury. True, it was a dead end – but if the monkey could cross the Thames, he could find a way out of here too.

"Peace, monkey," said Henry. He pointed to his chest. "I mean thee no harm."

"Ooh!" replied Banbury. He sounded quite cheeky.

Patience. Deliberate steps. Nothing to scare the monkey. It would all work out fine. And, as long as the monkey hadn't dropped more pages, Henry would return to master Griggs's shop and everything would be forgiven.

"OOH!" repeated Banbury, louder this time, and with a flash of movement began scaling the broken barrels that were piled behind him.

"No!" called Henry, forgetting his decision to take it slowly. He rushed for the monkey, scrambling over the wood, snatching at thin air where, seconds earlier, the monkey had been.

And at the moment Henry thought he might finally catch the animal, it leapt up onto a jutting window ledge. Open-mouthed, Henry watched as, from the window ledge, Banbury climbed the timber framing up onto the sloped, tiled roof above. A tile fell, speeding past Henry and smashing on the cobblestones below.

Grumbling to himself, Henry followed. For what else was there to do?

Tracing Banbury's path, he grabbed onto the window ledge and, with all the strength he had, hauled himself up. Hoping that nobody would open the window's wooden shutters, he shimmied across to the wooden timbers, just as the monkey had done.

"Oi! Get down, you little rat!" came a voice from below. But, unless it belonged to master Griggs, no voice would stop him chasing that thieving monkey.

Henry scraped his knees, his hands slipped from the wood, but, eventually, he pulled himself up and over the eaves. He stood now on a narrow wooden beam, chest level with the sloped roof. The street and the barrels seemed distant now, a dangerous drop below. And there, ahead, was Banbury – perched like royalty on a chimney pot, one hand clutching the stolen pages, the other a string of half-chewed onions.

"You, monkey," said Henry. "I've had it up to here with your onion-snatching, script-stealing tricks!"

Banbury, if he understood English, didn't appear bothered.

11. Rooftop rumpus

At the very top of the roof, where it came to a sharp upside-down "V", a long wooden ridge ran like a balance beam for anyone brave enough to try it. Or monkeys. Banbury scampered along the ridge, dropping onions as he went. The skins slid down the tiles and disappeared off the edge, down into the alleyway from where Henry had come.

Taking a deep breath, and trying to forget the height, Henry crawled up to the top, grabbing at the tiles and keeping his chest close to the roof. He moved slowly and, as he did, was conscious of how hot he felt. High above them, the sun shone down without mercy.

"You're not getting away this time," Henry muttered to himself but, in truth, he wasn't sure Banbury would even be there when he got to the top.

But he was and, if monkeys are capable of worry, he surely now looked anxious. Henry pulled himself up, straddling the beam like a horse, the rooftops dropping away on either side.

Banbury no longer gripped the papers. Instead, they lay on the beam, halfway between the two climbers.

"It's been good hunting, Banbury," said Henry. "But it ends now."

But Banbury was acting strangely. He appeared to be looking past Henry, at something over his shoulder.

"Ha!" said Henry. "I'm not falling for that. I'll turn, you'll grab the papers, and we'll be back on our merry chase once again."

Now the monkey pointed, frantically, with a tiny monkey finger.

"Enough! It's my first day at work – I'm not meant to be chasing monkeys over rooftops!"

And as Henry stretched out to grab the play, a voice called.

"Move not a muscle!"

Henry turned. And froze. A man was sitting on the same narrow ridge, nose red and eyes blazing. He recognised him from somewhere. His instruction was a little confusing. Should he continue to look over his shoulder at this bedraggled man? Must he really remain still?

"If this is your house – "

"I'm not here for conversation. Hand me that script and do it quickly," said Filbert.

There was a moment in which all three were sitting motionless. And then Banbury hopped towards the play. This was enough for Filbert to panic. Amazingly, like a street performer, he rose to stand on the beam, his arms extended for balance.

Henry hadn't come this far for some strange man to pinch the play at the last moment.
He stood too.

What happened next, happened quickly. Filbert tried to squeeze past, grabbing Henry for balance. Henry had nowhere to move, so resisted. They danced a little. And then an onion, conjured from somewhere, came spinning from Banbury's hand, past Henry's head, and directly into Filbert's face. Henry had thought the onions had gone. The monkey was full of surprises.

Naturally, Filbert looked confused and, in attempting to work out what had happened, stepped to the side. Unfortunately, here was only air. His feet went first, then the rest of him, bumping, sliding, flailing, down the Cheapside slope of the roof.

"I'll be revenged on the whole pack of youuuuuuuuuu!" he called, as he went.

There came a crashing of broken timber, out of view, and then voices.

"I'm fine, I'm fine," came Filbert's voice from down below. "I'm going home for a lie-down. I've a headache coming on."

Henry turned to Banbury. Banbury turned to Henry. The printer's apprentice was almost certain that the animal raised an eyebrow. And, as one, their glance fell on the manuscript, which remained between them.

They both darted at once. Banbury got there first. But Henry was a close second. Instead of paper, he grabbed fur. And instead of the security of the beam, he now found himself, and Banbury, rushing headlong down the other side of the roof, the smooth tiles sending them speeding like cannonballs.

They fell and fell and –

There was a brief moment when Banbury went slack in Henry's arms, and the boy wondered whether this was it. The end.

And what a way to go! Falling off a roof with a monkey. And *A Midsummer Night's Dream*.

Instead of striking cobblestones, however, Henry fell into something soft enough to cushion his fall. A straw-filled cart. His right knee and left elbow instantly called out in aching pain, but he was safe.

For a moment, all was still. Both monkey and boy were stunned. Then a slow voice said: "A boy and a monkey falling from the sky! Is this a dream?"

Pulling straw from his face and carefully straightening his back, Henry looked to see who had spoken. It was a worried-looking man with receding hair and a pointed beard. He wore the shimmering clothes of wealth.

The man bent over to retrieve a lost page of the play from the road. "This," he said, brushing dust from the page, "looks rather familiar. Yes. I do believe it's mine."

Banbury squeaked. Henry gulped.

For this was master William Shakespeare.

12. A twist in the tale

You might expect Henry to apologise or, at the very least, try to explain himself. Instead, he leapt out of the cart, screaming and brushing down his linen shirt. Shakespeare, it must be said, was a little confused. Banbury too, perched at the rear of the cart, looked to be frowning.

"Gah!" said Henry, jumping to the ground, arms flailing, narrowly missing one of the cart's wheels with his head.

"Young man! What's the matter? First falling from the sky, now this!"

Henry stopped. He was sure he'd seen not one, but two, huge bees. "I saw bees," said Henry, pointing towards the cart. "Two bees." His voice dropped at the clear lack of buzzing. "Or not two bees."

Shakespeare raised an eyebrow. "That," he said, "is the question." He held out a hand to help Henry get to his feet. "And there are others too. Such as: quite what is happening here? I was seeking a little peace and quiet, not easy in a city this loud. And, before I know it, a monkey and a boy are falling from the skies."

For a moment, Henry just stared at his legs. His heart beat doubly quick. This was supposed to be a simple delivery – his first proper task. And now? He'd had the pages stolen by a monkey, almost died, and made a fool of himself in front of the most famous writer in the country. What if master Griggs sent him packing? What if master Shakespeare had him hauled off to the constables for monkey-related crimes?

Henry blurted out the whole story – master Griggs, the missing pages, the monkey, the rooftop chase, the man following him – and a grin began to creep across the playwright's face.

"The player told me to pretend these are my grandmother's recipes," Henry added.

Shakespeare nodded. "I'll wager he did. And this monkey here was the culprit? The onion-loving thief?"

"That he was, master Shakespeare," said Henry, wincing. "He's called Banbury."

"Banbury," said Shakespeare.

What if the writer lost his temper, perhaps demanded payment, or stormed off to report them both? Maybe master Griggs would never print his plays again.

Henry didn't move. Every muscle was tight as rope. This was the moment at which his whole day, his whole life, might fall apart. He'd never felt such hatred towards a monkey. It was all Banbury's fault.

However, instead of fury, a slow smile spread across the playwright's face. "Quite the adventure you've had. Desperately fortunate, too, that this cart happened to be here. What a coincidence that it should be waiting in just the right place."

"Like in one of your plays, master Shakespeare."

"Well, I'm not sure I'd include a succession of such unbelievable events, but there we go."

Henry considered the plot of *A Midsummer Night's Dream* but decided to keep his mouth shut. Shakespeare seemed to be taking everything with good humour, and he didn't want this to change.

"Master Griggs will be waiting in the print shop and he'll already be wondering where I am. I promised my mother that I'd last longer than a day. I'll do well to survive until lunchtime as it is. What shall I do?"

"Don't fret. All's well that ends well," said Shakespeare. "Hmm. That's got a certain ring to it."

The playwright turned to Banbury and extended a hand. "The papers, please, Monsieur Monkey."

Banbury, hopping to the edge of the cart with the playscript, did as he was told.

Shakespeare flicked through the last few pages of *A Midsummer Night's Dream*. He added the spare paper to the end, then turned to address Henry. "You're missing much of this," he said.

"I've the rest here, master Shakespeare," said Henry, indicating his bag. His voice dropped. "Apart from the last page. It got a little wet."

Shakespeare's brow furrowed. He said nothing. He continued to stare at the stack of pages as if something precious had been ruined.

Henry's mouth went dry. He showed the writer the final page. It was impossible to read, just a blurred smudge of black ink.

"I tried drying it on a dog," said Henry.

Shakespeare closed his eyes. Henry could feel his stomach twist. He'd worked so hard to fix things – the running, the climbing, the monkey – and still it wasn't enough.

Then Shakespeare opened his eyes again and said: "Let's see what we can do." He cleared his throat.

"If we shadows have offended,

Think but this, and all is mended,

That you have but slumber'd here,

While these visions did appear.

And this weak and idle theme,

No more yielding but a dream,

Gentles, do not reprehend:

If you pardon, we will mend.

And, as I am an honest Puck,

If we have unearned luck

Now to 'scape the serpent's tongue,

We will make amends ere long;

Else the Puck a liar call.

So, good night unto you all.

Give me your hands, if we be friends,

And Robin shall restore amends."

"I'm sorry, master Shakespeare, but I don't understand."

Shakespeare took a long, deep breath, in the manner of an exasperated teacher. "It's the epilogue," he said. "The ending you're missing. How good is your memory? If you write it out before handing the manuscript in, nobody will know any better. Assuming you can write."

Henry nodded and Shakespeare recited the speech twice more, Henry following along, despite knowing for sure that he'd forget by the time he reached master Griggs's.

This completed, the playwright took a long hard look at Henry. "Do you know what I value most in a young man?" he asked. "Or an old man? Or a young woman? Or anyone?"

Henry thought hard. "A loud voice?" he said, finally.

Shakespeare smiled. "Imagination," he said. "And after imagination, courage. You, sirrah, have both."

Words failed Henry. His heart thumped so loudly he was sure Banbury could hear it. The country's greatest writer thought he had imagination. And courage.

"Thank you, master Shakespeare," he said, awkwardly. "I don't know what to say."

"Then write it down one day," said Shakespeare. "That's what writers do – when words fail them."

Henry nodded. He might just survive his first day.

Shakespeare turned to the cart and extended an arm. Banbury hopped on and, as if they were long lost friends, climbed up onto Shakespeare's shoulder.

"I've got just the part for our hairy friend here. Has there ever been a play with a role for a monkey before? I think not!" He tapped his forehead. "That's why I'm so highly rated! So now, you must excuse me. I've an actor to chase for selling off my work without asking permission. I'm sure he won't begrudge a couple of pounds. Adieu!" And, as Shakespeare wandered away, Henry could hear him muttering to himself. "To be or not to be? To be or not to be!"

13. Ink and applause

"You look like you've been wrestling a bear! What took you so long?" master Griggs exclaimed, when Henry finally returned to the print shop.

The shop felt like a stage before the curtain went up. It smelt, strangely, of burnt toast. The beater and the other pressman leant against the bench near the presses, arms folded, staring at the boy like he was a ghost.

"You take as long as you like, boy!" said Sam, the compositor. "I've never had such a calm start to the week."

It would be Sam's job to arrange the individual pieces of type – tiny metal blocks, each with a letter – into lines of text. It was skilled and meticulous work, not least because he had to work backwards as the type was reversed.

James, another apprentice, older than Henry, sniggered. "I'd have been back an hour ago if you'd sent me, master Griggs."

"Aye, but where were you when we opened up? Fast asleep still."

"Let's get on with it, then," said Ben, the beater. Peter, the other pressman, nodded.

Henry handed over the cloth bag. Griggs accepted it, pulling out the play. There was a clear distinction between the first three-quarters, which had remained safely stowed throughout the morning, and the last part, with which Banbury had been running around town.

Grunting, Griggs flicked through. When he reached the last page, he looked to Henry. "What's this? The hand is different."

Henry took a deep sigh, looked to his feet, and spoke quickly. "A monkey stole a bunch of pages and dropped the last one. But I caught him. And met master Shakespeare himself! He told me what to write, so I stopped at a stationer's stall and added it."

"A monkey?" laughed James.

Griggs shot him a look. James shut up immediately.

"I did my best, master Griggs."

Griggs nodded at Henry. "Your mother warned me about your imagination." Then he turned to Sam. "We'll start with the title page, Sam."

The letters were arranged in reverse, ink rolled onto the type, and the first sheet placed. Shortly, out from the press, a single, perfect page emerged. Henry stared, his mouth lolling. It was like some form of magic.

Griggs took the page and held it up high for inspection. Finally, he nodded. "Henry!" he called. The boy rushed to his side. Griggs handed over the page. "For you. A souvenir. Careful, though, it's wet." And, with quick fingers to his purse, pulled out two coins. "And these too. Anyone who fights a monkey and wins deserves a bit of silver." He looked Henry over. "And maybe a new shirt."

And as the day progressed, more and more printed pages came from the presses, the two apprentices hanging them to dry. And when the day ended, Henry looked to his ink-stained fingers and wondered how he'd made it through.

"Good work, Henry!" called Griggs, as the wooden shutters came down. "We'll make a printer of you yet. But less monkey business tomorrow, eh?"

Henry nodded, smiling. If this apprenticeship didn't work out, he could always become a writer.

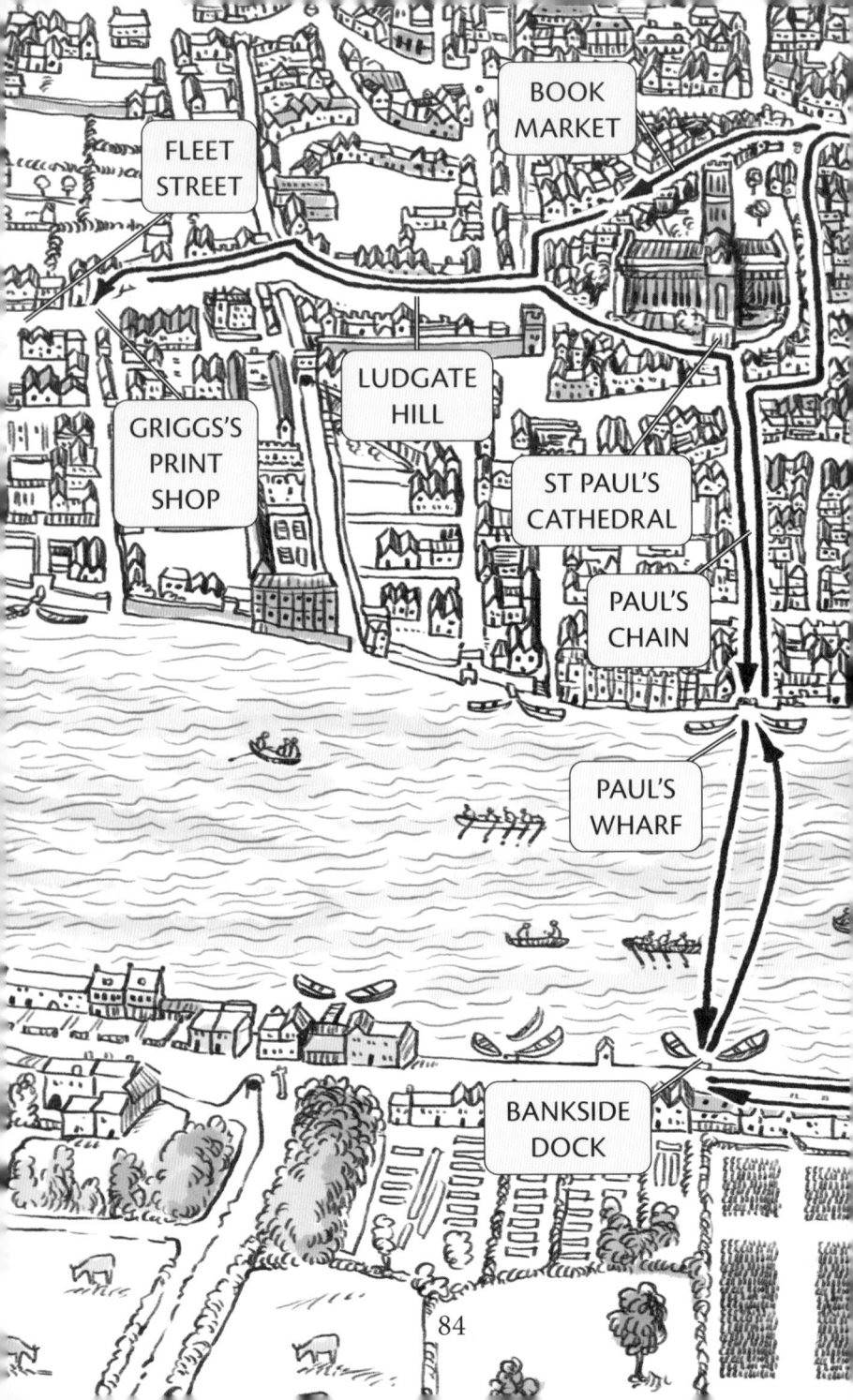

Book talk questions

What did you already know about Shakespeare before reading this book?

What was your favourite part of the story?

How do you think the process of printing a book is different now?

Would you have done anything differently to Henry?

Would you recommend this book to a friend?

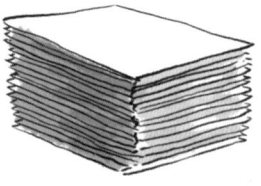

How did this book make you feel?

What was your favourite thing you learnt while reading the book?

How would you describe Henry, to someone who hasn't read the book?

Have you ever had to be responsible for something? How did it feel?

What three words would you use to describe the book?

Ask the author

What's your favourite Shakespeare play?
My favourite is *Macbeth*. I love the way it dives into questions of good and evil.

Tom Mitchell

Do you have any memorable moments from teaching Shakespeare in schools?
The comic parts of *The Tempest* are fun to teach. I think students expect it to be dry and dreary, but they often find it (or parts of it!) genuinely funny.

What do you think happens on Henry's second day at work?
I imagine he tries to keep a low profile. But it wouldn't surprise me if he spotted another monkey on the loose and ended up in more trouble before lunch.

How did you come up with the title?
The title's a nod to the old idea that if you gave an infinite number of monkeys an infinite number of typewriters, and infinite time, they'd eventually produce the complete works of Shakespeare!

Did you have any unexpected challenges while writing *Shakespeare's Monkey*?
The historical detail was trickier than I expected. Also, I didn't want full-blown Elizabethan language, but I did try to keep things from sounding too modern.

Did you learn anything surprising while researching the book?
Yes: bananas. They weren't really a thing in Elizabethan England. The first widely recorded sighting was in 1633 – even then, they were rare.

How do you think you would manage in Elizabethan London?
Honestly, not well. The smells alone would finish me off.

What's your favourite book with a historical setting?
As a kid, I enjoyed *The Eagle of the Ninth* by Rosemary Sutcliff.

How do you come up with your characters?
They usually begin with a voice. Once I can hear how they speak, the rest tends to follow.

Published by Collins
An imprint of HarperCollins*Publishers*

The News Building
1 London Bridge Street
London SE1 9GF
UK

Macken House
39/40 Mayor Street Upper
Dublin 1
D01 C9W8
Ireland

© HarperCollins*Publishers* Limited 2026

10 9 8 7 6 5 4 3 2 1

ISBN 978-0-00-878471-3

All rights reserved. No part of this publication may be reproduced, stored in a retrieval system, or transmitted in any form by any means, electronic, mechanical, photocopying, recording or otherwise, without the prior written permission of the Publisher or a licence permitting restricted copying in the United Kingdom issued by the Copyright Licensing Agency Ltd, 5th Floor, Shackleton House, 4 Battle Bridge Lane, London SE1 2HX.

Without limiting the exclusive rights of any author, contributor or the publisher of this publication, any unauthorised use of this publication to train generative artificial intelligence (AI) technologies is expressly prohibited. HarperCollins also exercise their rights under Article 4(3) of the Digital Single Market Directive 2019/790 and expressly reserve this publication from the text and data mining exception.

British Library Cataloguing-in-Publication Data
A catalogue record for this publication is available from the British Library.

Author: Tom Mitchell
Illustrator: Jon Davis (Advocate Art)
Publisher: Laura White
Commissioning editor: Holly Woolnough
Development editor: Zoë Clarke
Product manager: Holly Woolnough
Content editor: Selin Akca
Copyeditor: Sally Byford

Proofreader: Catherine Dakin
Reviewer: Lisa Davis
Fact checker: Sasha Morton
Cover designer: Sarah Finan
Internal designer: 2Hoots Publishing Services Ltd
Typesetter: David Jimenez
Production controller: Sophie Waeland

Collins would like to thank the teachers and children at Grange Primary School, Southwark, for being part of the development of Big Cat Read On.

Printed in the UK

MIX
Paper | Supporting
responsible forestry
FSC® C006032

Made with responsibly sourced paper and vegetable ink

Scan to see how we are reducing our environmental impact.

Get the latest Collins Big Cat news at
collins.co.uk/collinsbigcat

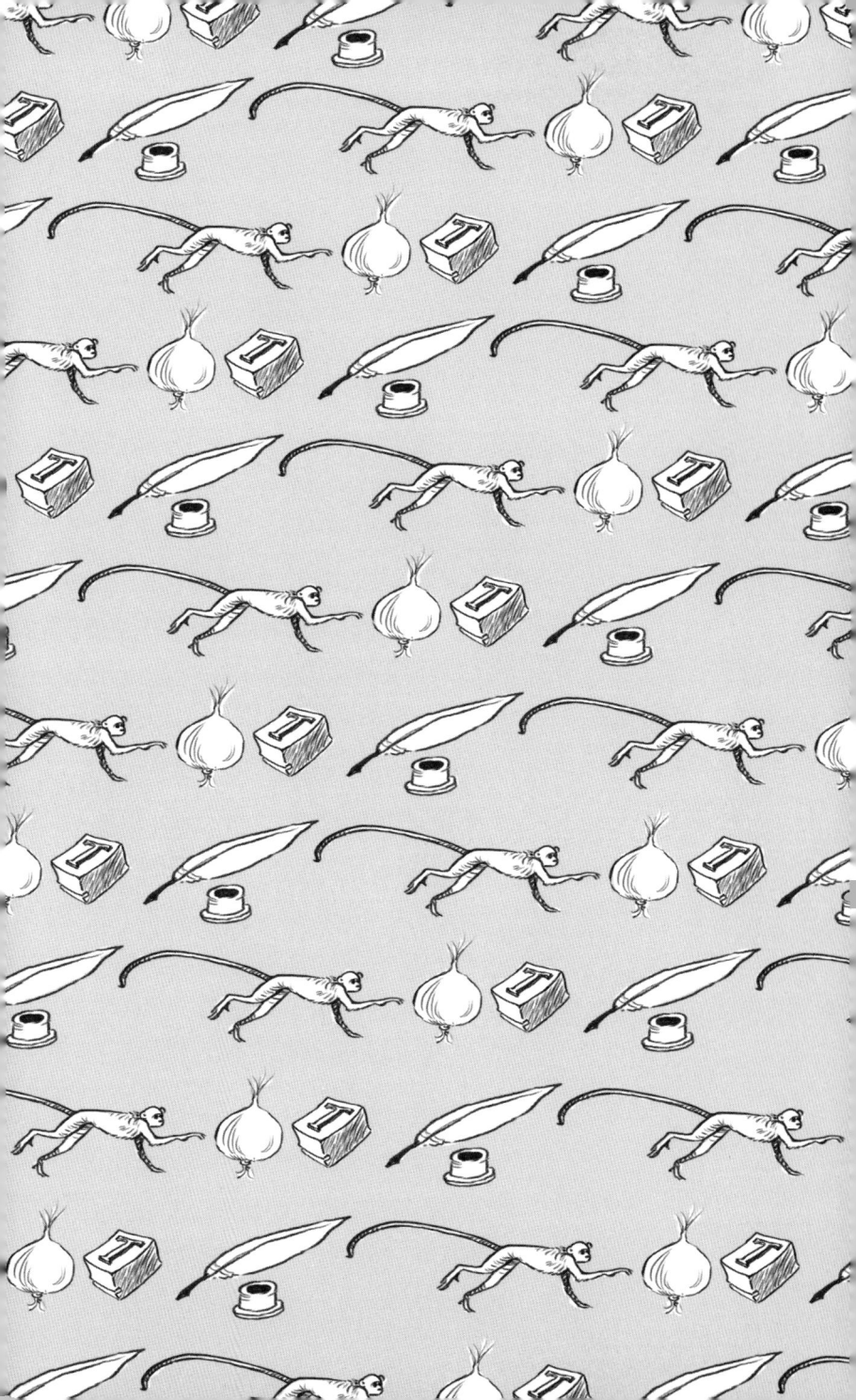

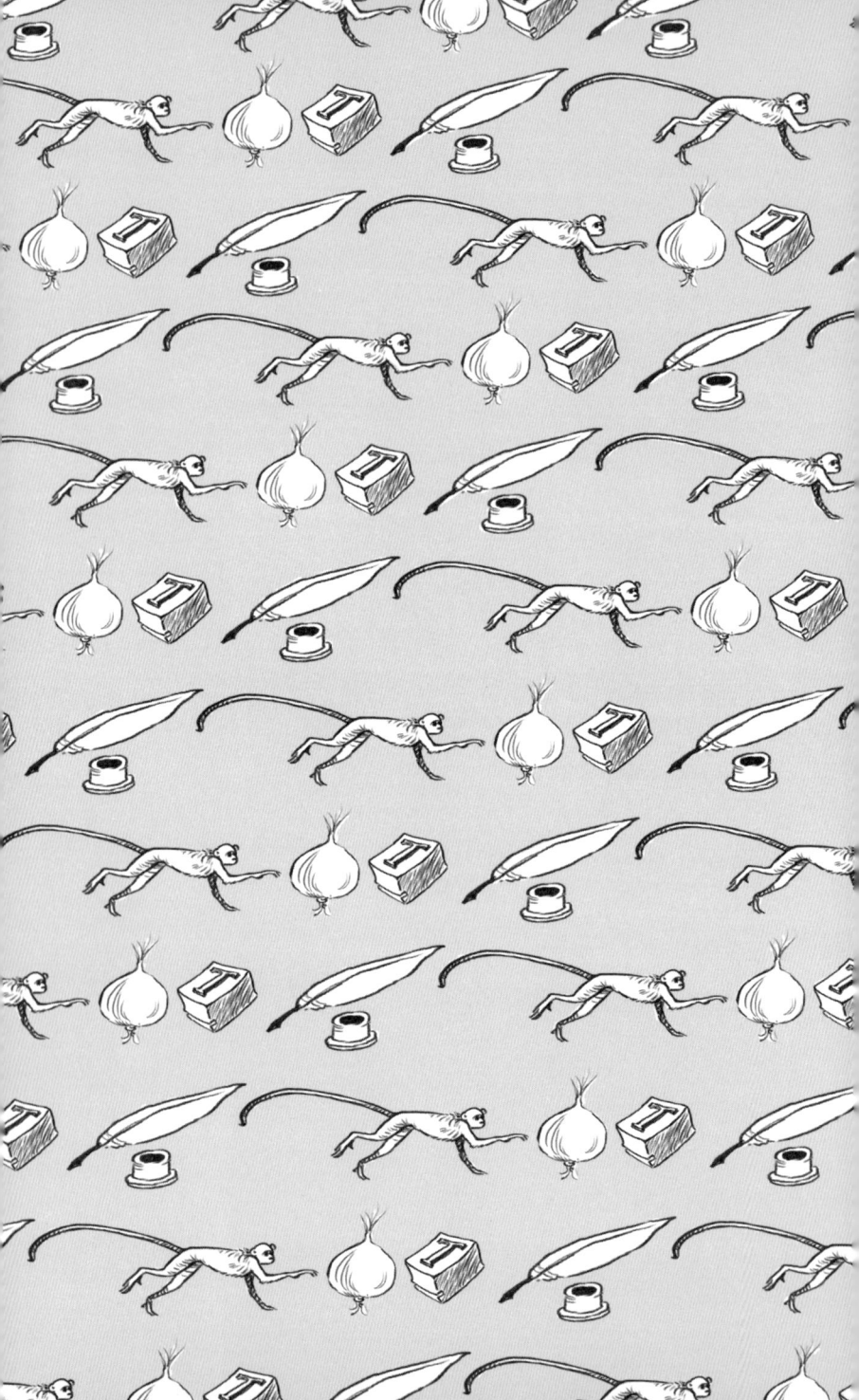